Fool in the Attic

ISBN: -13: 978-0615866826

Cover photo: Alicepopkorn (photoflickr)

Aldrich Press
24600 Mountain Avenue 35
Hemet, California 92544

Acknowledgments

Grateful acknowledgments are due to the editors of the following publications in which many of these poems first appeared:

Atlanta Review "Begging Bowl," "In Monet's Garden," "Suburban Vigilante"

Blue Unicorn "Marc Chagall Comes to Cupertino, California"

Bloodroot "Credo at 37,000 Feet" & "St. Crispen Avenue"

Buddhist Poetry Review "Beach Omen" & "Bluescape"

California Quarterly "5pm Cupertino," "A Kind of Pilgrimage," "Valley of Heart's Delight"

Chiron Review "Cat's Cradle," "A Delicate Point," "Elegy for Ben Kanter," "Holy Saturday," "Plebeian on the Front Porch," "Wild Kingdom"

Clare "The Skunks of Kingsbury Place"

Concho River Review "Transportation"

The Dos Passos Review "Phone Call from My Father"

Home Planet News "Pig in a Dutch Oven"

Iodine Poetry Journal "Graham Greene Fever Dream," "The River Guide as Marriage Counselor," "To Vincent on His 158th Birthday"

Main Street Rag "O Monster, My Monster!"

New Plains Review "October Song" & "Very Midsummer Madness"

Pearl "Amherst Clip Joint," "June 1," "Note from Pharaoh's Mother," "Watergate Summer," "Wrestling Satan"

Perspectives "Fool in the Attic"

Sojourners "Ode to St. Anthony of Egypt"

Spillway "Hamlet on the Ash Heap"

Suisun Valley Review "Little League"

The Sun "Christmas Eve, Almost Midnight," "My Sister's First Boyfriend," "Smog Baby," "Zen Cat"

Time of Singing "No Lights, No Siren" & "Theodicy"

Several of these poems appeared in the chapbook, *Plebeian on the Front Porch*, published by Finishing Line Press, 2012.

The author would also like to express his gratitude to Ken Weisner and Bob Dickerson for their support and editorial assistance in the creation of this book.

For seven inspiring teachers:
Richard Lee, Elliot Fried, Marilyn Johnson, Gerald
Locklin, Richard Lyons, John Haislip, Ralph Salisbury.

Fool in the Attic

poems by

David Denny

Table of Contents

I. An Otherwise Blue Sky

II. Suburban Vigil

III. A Heart Licked Clean

IV. Yawping with the Best of Them

V. Thirst No More

I. An Otherwise Blue Sky

St. Crispen Avenue

My mother screamed the day
the bees swarmed in our front yard.
She called my father at work to describe
for him the cloud of swirling honey bees
darkening the otherwise blue sky,
their low rumble like a lawnmower
engine running full tilt.

Later I learned that honey bees swarm
when they establish a new hive.
The queen had set up her court that day
in a corner of our house, over the garage.
One hour later, she was laying eggs
as her workers worked and her drones droned.
Around her they constructed her castle.

My father might have let them be
had they not begun to find their way
into my sister's bedroom through
the telephone jack. Even duct tape
couldn't deter them. We put our ears
to the wall just above the Barbies and
the Troll dolls to eavesdrop on their labor.

Weeks later, after the insecticide failed
to do anything but aggravate my asthma,
the beekeeper arrived in his white
space suit, netted hood, and smoke can.
He pried open the stucco wall and pulled
from beneath our eaves comb after gold-dripping
comb of the best honey we ever tasted.

I thought of them as Martian invaders.
But of course it was we who had
invaded the citrus groves of Brea, California.
After smoking the bees into a languid stupor,
the beekeeper removed the queen from her
throne room and easily packed away
in boxes her workers, drones, pupa, larva, eggs.

Four years later, I stood at that
patched corner of the garage as
the moving men loaded our boxes
of pots and pans, books and records,
clothing and toys aboard the Viking van.
It took only a few hours to empty
our beloved house of its belongings.

When our mother scooted into the
passenger seat of our station wagon,
our father followed the huge truck.
Through the rear windows my sister and I
watched orange trees, drive-in movie screens,
and the skeletons of new housing tracts
silhouetted against the otherwise blue sky.

Smog Baby

My father and I were hiking
up in the San Gabriel Mountains
where we'd been camping
for the weekend with Indian Guides.
We'd skipped some stones
across a lake, nibbled stale
sandwiches, climbed a few
trees, sung old songs around
a campfire. We all wore
decorated leather vests and
yellow headbands with fake
feathers in them. We all
pretended to know
something about the land.

As we began our descent
toward camp, my father halted
me by tapping my shoulder
and pointing out toward
the valley. For the first time
I noticed the thick brown
inversion quilt that smothered
the big arid valley we lived in.
"What *is* that?" I asked.
"That's what we breathe
every day," he said. The other
fathers and sons stopped too,
and looked out at the muck
that stretched from the foothills
all the way to the ocean.

Few of us ever saw much
of our dads at home, so
we didn't mind the phony

costumes. For once our fathers
didn't smell of aftershave;
they didn't lift the lid to piss;
they didn't backhand us
when we cussed. We were
men together, or so we thought.
We had one more terrific night
of ghost stories in sleeping bags
before we had to drive back
down into the land of mothers
and sisters, down there in
that thick goo that passed for air.

We looked out at it without
ever wondering how it got there.
Our fathers, of course, had
helped put it there. And later
we would help make it worse.
We would continue to drive
and smoke and work for
companies that belched chemicals
through smokestacks—
just as our fathers had.
But for this instant
we gazed out at it
in perfect ignorance.

Wrestling Satan

Like the criminals
Broderick Crawford
hunted down
on *Highway Patrol*,
he had more than one name:
Devil. Lucifer. Satan.
He looked like a
poorly-dressed Beatnik:
monochrome suit, goatee,
spiked shoes. He was
the opposite of Santa Claus:
pointy, mean, a taker.
In medieval paintings
he grabbed the ankles
of sinners and sucked them
through the floor
into a deep, dark place
with no TV and no candy.

One day he arrived
to take me. I stared him down
like The Rifleman
on Main Street.
I remembered the wrestlers
on TV—big bruisers
with thick necks and
bellies like the hoods
of old Buicks. They would
pick up their opponents and
slam them to the mat,
then bounce off the ropes
and flatten them,
lift their legs and

rock them back to
execute the inescapable
Boston crab.

So in the dirt patch
where we kept
the garbage cans
at the side of
our house, I threw
the devil against
the ropes, twisted his
sinewy arm behind
his back and,
when the referee
wasn't looking, stomped
on his spiked tail.
My plan was
to send him cowering
back to hell
empty-handed.

Thirty years of fighting
and he hasn't tired yet.

Little League

It was a windy, overcast day. Our small,
wiry team of eleven and twelve year olds
had been intimidated by a larger, better team.
By sheer luck we had held on to a one-run
tie into the last inning. Two outs.
Man on third. I had already whiffed
three times that day. I was afraid
of the fastballs the pitcher was whipping at us.
I expected to be humiliated this final time,
with the hope that our opposition would
put us out of our misery in the next half inning.

My batting helmet was too loose.
My socks drooped. I saw the wind-up
but I don't think I saw the pitch. I closed
my eyes and swung. The aluminum bat
awoke me with a loud *dink*. My hands
stung from the connection. I opened my
eyes and saw the ball drop into right field.
Almost as an afterthought, I tore off toward
first, getting there with time to spare.

My dad was the first base coach.
He slapped the plastic bill on the helmet,
dropping it over my eyes. "You did it,"
he said. "You won the game." I lifted
my helmet in disbelief. Soon the team
mauled me, slapping my back and shouting,
finally knocking me to the ground, then
lifting me to their shoulders. I remember
thinking, *I should close my eyes more often*.

My Sister's First Boyfriend

One summer my sister lost weight
       and grew boobs; her skin cleared up.
By fall she had a boyfriend—
       a tall, dark, skinny boy,
who sat with her for hours at
       a time on the diving
board in our backyard, making out.
       How boring, I thought. How
could someone stay interested
       in a kiss for so long?
I kept waiting for them to do
       something else. They kissed and
they kissed. Father was safely at work,
       where he sold steel and more
steel. Mother watched them from the kitchen
       window, where she peeled
potatoes and more potatoes.
       I watched from the window
in the back door to the garage,
       where I was busy curling
and curling a weight bar. My sister
       and her boyfriend, wrapped and
wrapped around each other like freezing
       people in a snow cave,
kissed and kissed on the wooden
       diving board my father
had sanded and sanded, then varnished
       and varnished. He had rubbed
that board for so long I thought he
       would reduce it to a
wafer. Why not buy a fiberglass
       board? I asked. No, he would
make this one like new. And on it
       sat my new sister with

her new boyfriend. As my mother
        scraped new potatoes. And
I contrived to grow new muscles.
        And my father filled orders
for girders to hold up new freeways.

Watergate Summer

So many flies on the window screens.
On the television, well, they call them
hearings: gavels insist upon the truth.
Names drawled from the tongues of senators:

Ehrlichman, Haldeman, Magruder, Mitchell,
Colson, Dean. And rising up behind them all,
a glorious American mongrel, the perpetually
angry uber-father, Mister 5 o'clock Shadow

Himself. He stands on the back stoop,
wagging his shoe at the whole country.
Heat waves billow. No more lemonade.
And the flies—did I mention the flies?

Truth hung out to dry on laundry lines.
The mushroom cloud meekly steps aside.
So much in this busted and cranky world
nevertheless shines like an unlikely star.

Catalina and Beyond

In Memoriam, Mahlon George Denny (1932-2004)

This memory just came floating back to me
across the years. Who knows how accurate it is?
Who's to say that it hasn't been worked over
by my subconscious and bubbled up
for some reason I can't now name?
The memory is of riding your back
out in the deep water beyond the breakers
in Huntington Beach. I was afraid of
the water, but you wanted me to overcome
that fear. You wanted me to see that *you*
weren't afraid. I clung to your shoulders,
dug my heels into your sides, and shivered.
The water beneath us was dark and full of mystery.
The blue sky overhead was vast and cloudless.
We could see all the way to Catalina Island.
As a kid, for two weeks, you had camped
in a tent on the beach there, looking through
binoculars with some of the other boys
at Errol Flynn's yacht anchored just offshore.
It was the best vacation of your life.

You moved through the water in a kind of
dog paddle so as to keep me well above
the surface. I could see mom on the blanket
back on the sand, turning over to even her tan.
Ahead of me in everything, sis swam nearby,
humming a tune from a movie we had seen
at the Surf Cinema that week. I begged you
not to swim too far. I knew there were rip
currents that could take us out, and with sixty
extra pounds on your back we wouldn't have
lasted long. I wanted to know how deep
the water was. You were trying to explain

that it didn't matter. If you knew how
to swim, you said, the depth of the water
was of no consequence. It could be
a thousand feet deep, you said, and you would
still make the same fluid motions with legs
and arms to stay afloat. How deep is it *here*?
I asked, teeth chattering. Only twenty or
thirty feet, you said. How many ravenous
creatures could fill the space beneath us?
I wondered. I clung to you like death.

I confess I'm still afraid of the water.
It isn't your fault. You did the best
you could. I never was as brave as you.
The ocean is dark and deep. The mermaids
sing to me, call me out beyond the waves.
There's nothing to fear, they chant. But given
the chance, they would grab my ankles and
take me down. Thirty-five years later
sis and I spread your ashes upon that water.
I imagine the particles of your body,
poured from the canister like so much coarse
sand across the dark surface, have drifted
easily to Catalina and beyond by now.
In a sense you are still out there, dog paddling,
whistling that Nat King Cole tune about those
lazy, hazy, crazy days of summer.
When I look out at the waves and the
horizon beyond that's how I imagine you.

Someday, I suppose, years from now, my own
son will be sitting alone somewhere
in the stillness of the evening when some
random memory of the two of us will pop

into his head. I hope he won't remember
the time I spanked him for mocking me.
I hope he won't remember the pettiness,
the insecurity, the ridiculous fears
that occupied so many hours of his
old man's life on earth. I hope he remembers
us hiking through the tall trees and stopping
for a drink of water and listening
to the woodpeckers knocking in the branches
overhead. I have a wonderful memory
of us walking out of the Stanford Theatre
one night after watching a couple of
Bogart movies while stuffing ourselves
on popcorn and candy and soda.
He was about the same age I was
when I clung to your back at the beach
that day. And strolling together out
into the cold night, he did the most
remarkable thing: he took my hand and
held it as we walked to the car together.
As a gentle rain misted the windshield,
I navigated the dark river of freeway
homeward. When he fell asleep in the seat
next to me, I remember praying,
Oh God, don't ever let me forget this.

A Delicate Point

Suburban kids on hot summer afternoons,
we chased down the ice cream truck and
lined up for red, orange, and yellow Rocket Pops.
After licking clean the wooden sticks, we
sat on the curb, sharpening them to a point
against the cement, stopping now and then
to feel the heat of the wood, the shiny
sharpness of the new edge as it emerged.
We turned our sticks from side to side,
rubbing them against the curb, and then lay
them flat to get the edges smooth all around.
We brought them each to a delicate point—
a small wooden knife. Why? It was something
to do. Miniature Jimmy Cagneys, we adopted
tough guy stances, circling one another until
our mothers on front porches called us home.

Years later, my wife's uncle, a guard in
a maximum security prison in West Virginia,
showed us a shiv he had recovered during
a routine search; it had been fashioned from the lip
of a fiberglass cafeteria tray and sharpened
by the same method we kids once used on
our popsicle sticks, only this one was wrapped
in duct tape for a death grip. He had discovered it
on top of a locker, before it could be used against
him or another guard or against another inmate.
He demonstrated the way the cons would tuck
the shiv up under a sleeve, come up close
behind the unwary victim, and thrust the blade
between the ribs. The killer could be halfway
across the yard by the time his victim dropped,
his blood-sputtering lips mouthing the word mother.

The River Guide as Marriage Counselor

As we climbed into the raft
our guide gave us the talk:
White water rafting, he said,
is the most exciting sport there is.
The thing to remember is that
it's all about peaks and valleys.
The peaks are thrilling and
the valleys are dull, but the key is
to see it all in one piece.
It's a Zen thing, he said.
He pushed our raft out into the current
and took his place in the rear.
Pointing us downstream, he said,
When I say *forward* that means
paddle together, in tandem, as a team.
Watch your partner. Row together.
When I say *back*, plant your feet
under the lip of the raft there and dig
the oar into the water like a shovel into gravel.
Lean into it hard. Lean from the hip.
When I say *stop*, he said, your oar
should be in the air—just like you're
raising your hand in school.
There's nothing to it, he said,
so long as you see whatever happens
as part of the same picture.
Watch the river. Be alert.
We were out into the middle
of the river now, floating calmly.
We could hear the rapids up ahead
like distant applause. He said,
When we hit the class fours and
I say *hang on,* I mean grab the handle
there and lean towards the center.

Two things will happen. When we top out,
he said, the river will lift our nose.
All you'll see then is the sky.
The thing to remember is
where there's a top there's a bottom.
And when we drop down
into the soup you'll feel a long slide.
All you'll see then is the foam.
Don't relax your grip during the slide
because you're about to hit bottom.
If you pop out of the raft, the icy green splash
will numb you if you let it. Don't.
Point your feet downstream, he said,
and hold onto your helmet.
The important thing is not to panic.
Keep your mouth closed. Breathe
through your nose. If you get sucked under,
he said, try to get a breath, relax, and
go with it. If you fight the current,
he said, you'll lose. This river has been here
longer than you, and this river will be here
after you're gone. He snapped
his helmet into place. Then he said,
Are there any questions?

Theodicy

We pulled over and stopped the car
along a high ocean vista on a bright
California morning, with gulls gliding overhead
and waves crashing on the rocks below.
My wife and I opened the car doors
to enjoy the freshness and stunning beauty.
We unfastened our three-year-old son from his
car seat and stretched our legs. Our son sat
in the dirt and gathered a few toys around him.
Suddenly, he tossed his rubber duck and it
sailed over the cliff. Then, before we knew it,
he ran after it. Diving, my fingers caught
his t-shirt two steps from the edge.
Flushed with adrenaline and a potent combination
of relief and dread, I strapped him back
into his car seat. Screaming for his lost rubber duck,
he kicked and tugged at the straps. His cheeks
reddened with anger. From his perspective,
salvation looked like undeserved punishment.
And because of his rage and tender youth,
I could not be justified in his sight.

Phone Call from My Father

Listen, I've got a confession to make.
I'm alive and well and living in Seattle.
It wasn't *my* heart that stopped;
that was some other sweet sap.
I slipped out the back door
of the ER, hailed a cab, hopped
a freight train, hitchhiked
the last few miles. I'm alive
and well and living in Seattle.
Tell your mother I'm sorry
for all the trouble. Did the insurance
cover it all? It wasn't *me* you
poured into the Pacific from the back
of your sister's boat; that was
some other poor bloke. So
the good news is, just as you'd hoped,
I'm alive and well and living in Seattle.

Belly Poem

Grandpa Mac's was volleyball-sized,
composed chiefly of Pabst Blue Ribbon
and chunks of Monterey Jack.

Uncle Bill's was an over-inflated basketball,
filled with iced tea and steak.
It entered the room before him.

My dad had the proverbial spare tire,
low on air. With his shirt off
it jiggled like Santa's jelly bowl.

Mine is more soccer ball than not—
firm and all out front. From behind
you might never know I had one.

Like Buddha's famous bronze protrusion,
my belly is here to stay.
Exercise and diet won't deflate it.

Maybe I should learn to celebrate it—
like Allen Ginsberg and his sphincter,
or Lucille Clifton and her big hips.

Go ahead and give it a good punch.
This belly's got style, baby.
This ain't no southbound belly.

II. Suburban Vigil

Plebeian on the Front Porch

The last rays of sunlight stretch across the lawn.
Angry scrub jays fill the trees with noise this evening,
scolding our cat, who sits on the front porch with me,
feigning innocence. There are only four or five of them,
but they cry out like a choir of demons tormenting

a damned soul in Dante's hell. Our cat has been feasting
on their young all summer long and they've had enough.
In recent weeks they have gone on the offensive,
swooping in like kamikazes to peck at her with their sharp beaks.
I have dabbed her wounds with hydrogen peroxide

and, like an old fight trainer in her corner, offered advice
on how to dodge them and swipe back with her claws.
It's a betrayal of the poet's pacifist code to confess
my partisanship, I know. According to ancient tradition
I'm supposed to praise the beauty of the birds

and the delicacy of their song, to decry the cruelty
of our predatory nature as symbolized by my cat.
I swear if they were doves or sparrows or purple martins
I would urge diplomacy, but the cries of the scrub jays
are so offensive that I am glad to root for the brutal kill.

Scooping what's left of their small corpses onto the spade,
I have found myself lecturing them on the way to the garbage can:
"If you only knew when to keep your mouth shut,
it might not have come to this." A little later,
when the sky has darkened and the yellow moon

charges the raucous jays to settle into their nests, my cat
will curl herself into a harmless ball at the foot of my bed,
and the crickets will call a truce. Like a sleepy crowd
huddled around the piano of Hoagy Carmichael,
they will croon us up the lazy river toward our dreams.

The Skunks of Kingsbury Place

The sound of my car at the curb sends them
scattering, tails aloft, scent glands sputtering.
The call goes out among them: false alarm,
only the human returning to his nest. They
resume their foraging over in the cul-de-sac
beneath the blood-red midsummer's moon.
A lingering tang drifts through open windows
and haunts us through the restless night.
We turn and turn upon our flowered sheets.
In the morning we emerge with caution
and pause to think of them snoozing
among the Hydrangeas next to the mailbox.
Our human defenses are less pungent but
no less intense. On occasion the instinct
to fight or flee fills the air between us
with ancient suspicions. Mostly, though,
we side by side gather and feed, nest and mate,
play and rest—a peaceable kingdom in which
we keep our distance, rear our young, and
honor our dead. And this other instinct—
that prompts us to record this fragile compact
composed of one part fur and teeth and claws
and another part cunning and wit and luck—
is it mere glandular reflex or rather divine burden?
The skunks of Kingsbury Place aren't telling.
They stir only a little in their sleep and
only then to give each other room to dream.

Very Midsummer Madness

The fat, slow, yellow-armored Junebugs
appear at our kitchen window by night
every Independence Day weekend.
Are they also stupid? They seem so.
Keystone Kops of the insect world,
they bump into nearly everything.

In their constant and pathological
longing for light, they hit the screen,
drop on their backs to the sill below,
wiggle their tiny legs until they starve.
I once saw hundreds of them roiling
in a public Jacuzzi, like beetle soup.

The pool boy scooped and scooped
them with his skimmer. Still they
kept coming, undeterred by the floating
corpses of their kin swirling in the hot,
frothy water, silhouetted by the floodlight
illuminating our pale legs and feet.

Oh, sweet, silly Junebugs, counter-
kamikazes, you die not to bring honor
to your ancestors or descendents but
only for mad love—over the top,
out of control, gotta have it, take me Jesus
love—of that wonderful, hypnotic light!

Marc Chagall Comes to Cupertino, California

Until Chagall set up his easel in my backyard,
I hadn't noticed the depth of blue swirling in our sky.
Until that strange little man called Chagall came,
I never realized how many angels we had hiding

in the tomato bushes. (No wonder they're so delicious!)
What an impoverished life I led before Chagall
cried, "How can a man live without chickens?"
And now a flaming red rooster hides in the plum tree.

Until Chagall showed up with his palate in hand,
I never saw how much my meager barbeque
resembled the Ark of the Covenant, never knew
that my cat was really a sphinx, never heard the orchestra

tuning its instruments within our redwood fence.
See how my wife now flies above the rooftop!
Look—the smoke curling from the chimney resembles
a chorus line of Cossacks dancing the Troika.

Until Chagall set up his easel in my backyard,
I mistook this hot bed voodoo lounge at the center
of the hyperventilating universe for a bland little house
in a bland little suburb in the big bland state of California.

Wild Kingdom

This morning I set a glass
into the kitchen sink, startling
my cat on the back porch.

She was crouched over
her kill—a scrub jay who dared
swoop one too many

times across her lawn.
Her eyes dropped back
to the object of her study.

This afternoon my student stops
writing her exam to stretch
and look out the window.

Somebody in the back row
clears his throat. Taking up
her pen again, her eyes

drop back to her prey.
She tears another bite
from under its wing.

October Song

All over the valley crows call to us;
mornings before work, standing in driveways,
sipping the last of the coffee, they call to us;

walking to the office or unloading groceries,
watering the flowers in the deep afternoon,
rooting at our daughters' soccer games, they call to us;

they call from treetops, television antennas,
random fenceposts; sitting on front porches,
lost in our evening reminiscences, they call to us all.

Dark evangelists, they carry bad news:
winter approaches, sickness lurks, death
awaits us all. Make a puny fist; shake it at the sky.

Suburban Vigilante

I'm driving to pick up my daughter from soccer practice
on a beautiful autumn evening with the darkening sky above
stippled by rain clouds and with orange leaves blowing
across my path and with the troubled sounds of Mahler
on the radio. I'm passing lawn sign after lawn sign advertising
that once again Richard Lee is running for mayor.
For the first time in my life I have an urge to own a rifle;
I would very much like to drive through town shooting holes
in Richard Lee's lawn signs. To be perfectly honest I care nothing
for Richard Lee and his endless campaigning for mayor.
I'm upset because my friend Ben lies in the hospital
with stage four lung cancer. Only a few weeks ago
he was cracking bad jokes at my office door, bravely rooting
for the Detroit Tigers, and now, damn it, I can't believe my friend
    is dying.
I've seen so much of death in the past three years I want to puke.
Richard Lee, I promise to vote for you if
you will use your newly-elected powers to detain Death
as an enemy combatant, ship him off to Guantanamo.
Death, you brown-toothed son of a bitch, when you come for me
you'd better first brush up on your smooth talking.
You'd better be wearing your best suit with your shiniest shoes.
You'd better slick that hair back out of your rotten yellow eyes
because right after I pick up my daughter from soccer practice
    today
I'm going to buy a rifle. You'd better start watching your back.
Hear what I'm talking about? Just as soon as I aerate
some of these Richard Lee lawn signs, I'm coming gunning for
    you.

Elegy for Ben Kanter

Stepping outside after the first good rain of autumn,
I smell wood smoke from a neighbor's chimney
as I survey the garden. The apple tree is loaded this year
like never before. Its dappled fruit has been washed clean
by this morning's downpour. I pick one and bite into its
crispy-juicy goodness. Even though they are nearly finished,
the big orange, red, and yellow Dinner Plate Dahlias sparkle
and sway. Heavy with raindrops, they bow in my direction.
The Aztecs used to eat the giant flowers and make pipes
from the stems. I will wait until they lay completely drained
of beauty, then pull them up by the roots and toss them
into the yard waste bin. As I do this I will say to myself,
I should eat these flowers, I should make pipes from these stems.
My thoughts are heavy with Ben today, my friend
who lies on his deathbed in Good Samaritan Hospital.
When I visited him this morning, I had to do all the talking.
He was finished. Nothing left to say. I jabbered about how
he wasn't missing much at work, about the lovely view
of the foothills from his fifth-floor window, about
how lucky he was that his ex-wife Lucy was there
to pinch him and give him a hard time. When I left
it was with an awkward wave. I told him to hang in there.
I told him I would check in with him later. But what I wanted to
    say was
Ben I'm sorry you're leaving. I'm going to miss you, brother,
especially on days like this one, with Dahlias to look at
and apples to taste and wood smoke to smell. I'll think of you
each year in the freshness that follows autumn's first good rain.

Gratitude in Swing Time

for Jill

November again. How did it happen? Yesterday was May.
My wife and I hiked out to the pond. Quail pranced and
paraded along the edges of the path. Young rabbits ignored us
and munched the new grass. A doe and her two fawns
came gently to drink, watching us watch them from the bridge
above the spillway. Water splashed down the boulders below—
the mouth of the creek. The blue jays scolded us for trespassing.
It was warm enough I slipped off my shirt and tucked it
into the pocket of my shorts. Our boots were coated
with the red dust of a lovely spring. We shoved handfuls
of trail mix into our mouths and washed the savory sweetness
down with cool water. May, it seemed, would never end.

Now here it is November. Were we to trudge out to it today,
we would find the edges of the pond parched and cracked,
all the animals in retreat. Suddenly the days are short and
we don't feel like doing much of anything. One of the sprinklers
in the corner of the lawn is broken. Water pools and floods
into the gutter. The once-purple leaves on the Japanese Maple,
golden last month, have now turned brown; they drop before our
        eyes.
All around us life is growing dim. To top it off, it's election
season again. The men in suits have trotted out their speeches,
and once more we play at democracy. Surviving soldiers
have come home to headaches, nightmares, and unemployment.
A lone gopher has ceased his campaign against our snapdragons.

November: month of long shadows. Even your stars streak
hurriedly across the night sky as if in a rush to escape the galaxy.
December will soon arrive, bags dangling from her arms,
step hobbled by a broken heel, wig off-kilter, a long pink strand
dangling in her eyes. On the evening news, anchors recite
the old familiar platitudes; the faux windmill in our neighbor's

backyard spins first one way, and then another. It is one thing to say we will remember May, yet another to say that May will come again. So let us feast and drink the sweet wine made from grapes that grow on hillsides above the pond. It is only that trifle Time, after all. Let us raise our goblets and be truly thankful for the gifts we are about to receive.

Christmas Eve, Almost Midnight

Driving through the mist after delivering
packages, I come upon a family of deer
walking down the middle of the street.
I cut my lights and engine and coast
behind them a while. They are cruising
the neighborhood, nibbling the frosty lawns,
looking for Nasturtiums. I glide behind them
around a corner and down another street,
the only sound the crunching of newly-formed ice
beneath my tires, until they disappear onto the dark,
soggy soccer fields of the middle school.
I tell you I can count on one hand
the number of times I've been happier.

5pm Cupertino

I'm sitting in Peet's with my usual Cappuccino, reading.
I stop for a sip, trace the rim of the cup with my finger,
look out the window at Stevens Creek Boulevard.

Across the street cars are pulling in and out
of the Whole Foods parking lot. The construction workers
who were tearing up the road when I arrived

have collected their orange cones and gone home,
leaving their gashes in the asphalt covered with large
metal rectangles. The sun is making its final effort

to illuminate the world for another day. The foothills
above town are ready for Cézanne to come along
and capture the geometry of dusk. Suddenly, light

catches the trees along the sidewalk for a moment.
Though the top branches are bare, a few amber leaves,
still clinging to lower branches, shimmer.

I take another sip, grateful for the way the milk
and the espresso both calm and excite the nervous system.
With my glasses off, the cars resemble logs

being carried by a river current and the leaves
look like fuzzy yellow stars and the foothills—
I'll leave the foothills to my friend Cézanne.

Between Breeding and Feeding

In winter, on their long annual trip from Baja to Alaska,
gray whales will occasionally take a right turn into Monterey,
Half Moon, or San Francisco Bay. Mothers and calves mostly.
Adult males can't be bothered with side trips into dark,
shallow waters, only to be gawked at by lollygagging humans
hanging their puffy, cold faces over the railings of bridges
and wharfs to get a good look at them. They do draw a crowd,
these wayward mamas and their white-mottled babies.

San Francisco is the grander diversion, involving a hard right
turn against strong outgoing Farallon currents. Once inside
the Golden Gate, they must dodge barges, tugboats, and
Navy frigates. Soon sailboats and yachts crowd them until
the Coast Guard boys insinuate themselves into the parade.
The Blue and Gold ferries hang behind Alcatraz to let them pass.
Tourists hop off cable cars, point their cameras at water spouts.
Even the cynical sea lions on Pier 39 quit their barking.

Great bespeckled humps rise like jewel-encrusted hilltops,
then sink and rise, sink and rise—mama and calf out on a lark,
a little holiday from the more serious business of migration,
a little sightseeing excursion into the warm, polluted waters
beneath the twinkling lights and buzzing, sputtering, galumphing
city of landlubbers. Soon they turn, like synchronized jumbo jets
or a pair of 18-wheelers in a road ballet, and glide back out
with the tide, their internal compasses turning them true north.

Is it just our imaginations or do they really roll on their sides
and wink at us cheering them from the edges of the tall red
bridge? Happy for their progress but sad to see them leave,
we wave in frantic pulses, blessing them for blessing us,

as if they could hear us from our desolate height, we who
also sing for consolation and dream of the great pilgrimage,
the glorious feast in the icy depths, our huge, knuckled backs
coiling upward before the ultimate, unfathomed descent.

Holy Saturday

for Stephanie Timms

I am driving home from the local Safeway
with an Easter Lily in the passenger seat.
I pass the Alameda Family Funeral Home.
Several dark-clad staff members have just
emerged from the smoked-glass doors.
Like a team of Hamlets, they huddle briefly
in the center of the parking lot before scattering
in twos and threes and climbing into black cars.
Dispatched to the far corners of our valley, they
attend to those who would rather be doing anything else.

I pull into Peet's for a cup of steamed milk, espresso,
and sugar. Will it bring solace for my own grief,
or is such solace mere illusion? There is something
about sitting and scribbling among strangers,
a classical soundtrack drifting through the speakers,
a bulwark of sorts against inner darkness. Stopped
at a red light, I look up at the hills, shrouded in low clouds.
My heart beats an irregular rhythm. It flutters
like a bird against a cage that is too small.
Sometimes my medicine works, sometimes it doesn't.

A friend writes that she is paving the road to hell.
But the road to heaven appears to be all loose gravel.
We both travel tentatively, hoping we've made
the right turns. Pulling into my driveway,
I imagine the funeral directors arriving at their destinations,
bringing such solace as they are able. Inside,
the house is warm but empty. So I sit here in the car,
Easter Lily in the seat beside me, and look again to the hills.
There it goes again: the fluttering in my chest. Sometimes
the medicine works, sometimes it just damn well doesn't.

Valley of Heart's Delight

All over town
the plum trees
are in bloom.

Tender clusters
of white lace
announce that

Spring has purchased
her ticket, stands
now out on

the platform. She'll
soon be steaming north
on the Panama Express.

We will pull on
our short pants
and t-shirts

to greet her
at the station.
Here you are,

whisper the plum
trees, have yourself
some beauty, some

new life. Have
some warmth and
a little tenderness.

We pull on our
baseball caps and
breathe deeply,

gratefully filling our
lungs with the sweet
oxygen of mercy.

III. A Heart Licked Clean

Beach Omen

Walking along the
sand, the couple
pass a vulture perched

atop a shark carcass,
eye socket empty.
Later, on the way back,

the vulture is gone,
and the shark now lay
split from jaw to gills.

"Look!" She points
to its pink heart—
exposed, intact,

not yet fly-ridden.
"How to divine that—
are we more vulture

or shark, more air
or sea, scavenger or
predator?" He scoops

his fingers through
the wet sand,
opens his fist.

A sand crab
answers for him,
digging backwards

and downwards
against his flesh,
tickling his palm.

Sibling Sky

With the stern
yet beneficent
face
of the elder
brother,
the evening sun
turns in our
direction.
We avoid
his direct gaze
but never
ignore
his presence.
His deep
amber glow
advises but does
not admonish.
We love him.

In another
part of the
sky,
sister moon
slowly makes
herself known,
demure
above the
treetops, as
brother lounges
now beyond
the hills.

Oh, sister,
under your spell
we spin slowly
in place, like
gyroscopic
tops.

Fog City Doppelganger

On a street corner in the Tenderloin
a homeless man with three remaining

teeth and the breath of an open
grave wishes a savvy tourist

happy new year. He asks for
spare change, though he knows

this tourist will not produce any.
Nevertheless, he does succeed

in awakening in the tourist's mind
his other life, the one he might

possibly be living had he (instead
of her footman) become Fortune's fool.

The light changes from red to green.
The tourist crosses safely back into

his own life. But standing on the opposite
corner he briefly dreams himself drugged,

hustled into the hold of a tall Clipper
bound for Shanghai. A trolley bell calls him

back to his own century. He touches his
hip pocket, traces the edge of his

fine leather wallet, a portable womb
capable of birthing a series of other lives,

all equally brimming with promise.
He looks back across a wave of traffic,

sees the man stooped at the curb—
has he fallen? No, he cups his hands

around the small fire of a half-smoked
cigarette, the woman who tossed it into

the gutter steps quickly off the
curb, high-heeling in her own direction.

'Burb Rage Redux

He is behind a car he doesn't recognize.
The driver, a woman he's never seen before,
slows dramatically. She thrusts her arm

out her window and pumps her middle finger
at the sky. As he passes her, he sees
her red face, her angry tears, her lips

mouthing, "Go fuck yourself you fucking
asshole!" Her finger is still pumping
toward the sky. It is early on an otherwise

calm summer's evening. Who does she think
he is? What does she think he's done?
He turns a corner and never sees her again.

Random moments in his life, while shuffling
a deck of cards or watering the front lawn,
the specter reappears, vivid and startling as

on that long gone summer's evening,
prompting the ancient prayer of examen:
of what secret crime does he stand accused?

Postmortem Java

A mother and son went to a coffee shop.
They ordered great big porcelain mugs

filled to the brim with strong black coffee.
They sat across from each other next

to the window. Outside was a parking lot.
Cars edged in and out of spaces. They talked

into the afternoon, idle talk, talk of
little consequence. The son took his

cell phone out of his pocket, aimed it
at his mother, and took her picture.

Today, six years after her death, she
looks at him from across the small table,

a half-smile on her face, a great big mug of
steaming black coffee within reach.

Euro Mementos

Shifting the contents of the satchel he uses
to carry books and papers from class to class,

he startles a bug beneath the folds
near the seams. He drops the satchel

face open and out tumbles three big
cockroaches. They have hitched a ride

all the way from a seaside abbey in Normandy
to the new world. Colonizing his office,

they scatter and settle behind a filing cabinet.
He must remember to drop a few crumbs

of Parisian bread, now and then, tidbits
of soft cheese, perhaps an apple core to remind

them of home. He mayhap don a cowl
and chant faint hymns to the pale moon.

Splash Please

With 20,000 wayward
pieces of space debris
orbiting the earth,

something reenters
the atmosphere
about once a year.

No big deal. Yet.
Today is the day
the six-ton NASA

satellite comes
crashing through.
Driving in his quiet

suburban neighborhood,
he can't help but
glance at the sky

now and then.
Surely the chance
of anything

landing on his car
is remote. Ocean,
he almost prays,

you are so vast.
Big blue catcher's
mitt. Dearest ocean,

do your job.
Protect us, please,
from ourselves.

Aerial Prattle

Half a dozen crows
have decided to
persecute a hawk.

They cut sharp
patterns in the sky
around him

as he glides.
When he perches
atop a tall pine,

they hector and
ridicule him
like a gang

of Harpies. Thinking
to dethrone him, they
continuously

swoop and heckle.
He stares beyond them,
these mere scavengers,

spotting a field mouse
half a mile away.
When he finally lifts

and soars imperiously
toward the meadow,
all the crows can do

is chase behind,
cursing him
like jilted lovers.

Bluescape

In soil
turned
to mush

by weeks
of constant
rain, the

roots of
the grand old
California

Oak give
way. It
falls

across the
boulevard,
stops traffic,

and opens
a fresh piece
of sky.

Freud Bloom

A pink-tinged
yellow rose

blossomed
yesterday. Today

he sticks his
nose in it

and inhales.
He closes

his eyes as
when kissing.

When he
opens them

a honey bee
crawls out

from between
the petals

and mounts the
tip of his nose.

Flea Meds

Once a month he stalks his cat,
sneaks up on her from behind.

It's the only way to get it done.
He pins her head and hips,

parts the fur on the back
of her neck, squeezes

the tiny tube, releasing
the foul-smelling gel

to her skin. She yowls
at him, turning, and leaps

for the gap in the sliding
glass door. It'll be midnight

before she returns,
curling at his feet,

her tail whipping
against him, the oily spot

on her neck a mark of
her shame, his betrayal.

Zen Cat

When he opens
the door his
cat slips between

his legs, as
she does every
morning, trots to

the kitchen, where
she curls in
her usual spot

beneath the table
in a shaft
of sunlight slanting

through the blinds.
On the welcome
mat she has

left him a
bluebird's spindly legs,
tailfeathers, a heart

licked clean as
a smooth brown
stone. Wake up!

IV. Yawping with the Best of Them

Amherst Clip Joint

Walt Whitman climbed up into Emily Dickinson's
barber chair. She spun him 'round, then began
by tossing his great hat aside and pulling back
his wild hair. She twisted it into a ponytail and
pinned it atop his bumpy head. Then she went to
work on his beard—first with a pair of scissors
and second with the electric clippers. He closed
his eyes the way he did when he rode the ferry.
The straight razor hummed up and down the strop.
How many delicate strokes to unbeard a bard?

You should have seen him preen in her lavender-framed
mirror, turning his newly-naked face from side
to side and crooning, "You, madam, are an American
Delilah: by you I am sweetly and utterly undone."
To which she replied: "Look, Sam, that'll be two bits.
Don't trip over the lilacs on your way out the door."
At this he tossed back his head, opened his throat,
and yowled like a coyote in heat. Oh, that man could
yawp with the best of them! Only Dizzy Gillespie,
Joe DiMaggio, and Gary Cooper even came close.

Call him a barbarian if you must. But he sat most
daintily in Emily's chair that day, finally choosing
a red lollipop instead of bubble gum from the big jar
next to the cash register and then skipping down
Main Street's sidewalk toward the town's only saloon.
Some say that on a quiet day you can still hear the bell
over the door clanging out his farewell. I know
what you're going to ask: yes, she slapped his cheeks
gently with a little Old Spice before lowering his chair
and shaking the whiskers from the striped cotton apron.

June 1

On this day were born Marilyn Monroe
and Brigham Young. At first you think,
what strange astrological bunkmates: the notorious,
deeply insecure movie siren and the pioneering,
rigid moralist on a nationalistic mission
to establish America's own Jerusalem.
But then you see the logic: Here is a truly
American Gothic couple, minus the pitchfork
and the yawning carpenter house in the background.
Nothing sells more tickets, said that great American
pitchman, Cecil B. DeMille, than sex and religion.
How many wives did Young have?
Wikipedia says 55. And he sired 56 children.
Clearly the man had little need for Viagra.
Before the beard, he resembled Clark Gable.
How many bed partners had Marilyn? The count
varies according to biographer. Apparently
she never lacked lovers, only true love.

Something tells me that if Norma Jean Baker
had been born on the plains in the mid-19th
century, she might've been among Young's
traveling harem. Imagine the swinging hips
and heaving bosom of *The Seven Year Itch*
bound and gagged by a wool frock, the peroxide blond
hair held captive beneath a starched linen bonnet.
And how might Mormon doctrine have been altered
from this coupling? Would Young, like DiMaggio,
have sworn himself to Marilyn forever, forsaking
the 54 others? Or, like Kennedy, would he have
kept her as his own little executive privilege, supplied her
her own private Prairie Schooner and deaf, mute maid?

Think of their progeny. The wilderness might've
been cleared and peopled in half the time!
What sort of secrets would the famous desert temple
now hide? What gorgeous, devout giants might have
slouched towards Salt Lake City to be born?

O Monster, My Monster!

for Lawrence Ferlinghetti

The theorizing and calculating done, the stocking
of the laboratory and the positioning of the equipment
complete, the wickedly smart young Doctor Frankenstein
dons his lab coat and presents his servant with a gruesome
shopping list. Fritz, not Igor, hobbles out into the great
American graveyard at midnight with a spade in one hand
and a burlap sack thrown over his hump to collect
the ingredients his master would soon confect.
His way lighted by a gibbous moon, Fritz, not Igor,
digs up the broad shoulders of John Kennedy, the oversized
balls of Lyndon Johnson, the five o'clock shadow of
Richard Nixon, Gerald Ford's tremendous feet,
Jimmy Carter's Howdy-Doody grin, Ronald Reagan's
Vitalis-perfect hair, Bush the Elder's defective brain,
Bill Clinton's bulbous nose, Bush the Younger's
beady little eyes, and Barak Obama's elephantine ears.

Back in the stone laboratory, the young doctor assembles
the presidential parts into a slightly green amalgam
now laid out upon the gurney, its hulking corpse
complete with trademark flat head and neck electrodes,
the badly-tailored, apparently colorless suit, the huge
black boots. The whole mad contraption now rises
as Fritz, not Igor, madly turns the crank and it rises,
madly rises toward the storm. The laboratory is animated
by arcing electrical charges. Sparks reach across impossible
distances; the tremulous music of hubris harmonizes
with the storm. And as the large stitched hand
of the corpse twitches with life, the mad young genius,
his hair on end, opens his throat and cries, "It's alive!"

And the monster, like Herman Munster on ecstasy,
sits straight up with a dazed look, composes itself,
the edges of its thin presidential lips forming a goofy grin.
"I do solemnly swear," recites the hulking monster,
"that I will faithfully execute the office of President
of the United States," as Fritz, not Igor, and the doctor,
cower in the corner, "and will to the best of my ability,
(it clears its throat) preserve, protect and defend (it stands
full height with hand on heart) the Constitution of the United
    States."
Fritz, not Igor, is the one who immediately understands
that the monster is a mistake. The young doctor is too much
in love with his creation to see that he has reanimated
a megalomaniac. As he guides the monster to the dungeon
and locks it in irons, Fritz, not Igor, hears it muttering
angrily under its rancid monster breath about the Bay of Pigs,
the Gulf of Tonkin, Watergate, Billygate, the Iran-Contra Affair,
the pardon of Nixon, the invasion of Panama, Monicagate,
phony weapons of mass destruction, and bail-outs, bail-outs,
bail-outs. The monster becomes increasingly agitated,
tyrannical blood boiling in its cobbled veins, the angels
of its better nature thoroughly subdued by hyper-patriotism.

Fritz, not Igor, decides the monster must be put down.
He brings on the firey torch, his own version of water-boarding,
but the flames only aggravate and empower the monster,
who breaks its bonds, strangles Fritz, not Igor, and shuffles
out into the fresh morning air, its metallic Johnsonian
gonads clanking, its perfect Reagan hair not moving
in the summer's breeze, its Gerald Fordian feet tripping
over each other, its beady Bush the Younger eyes squinting
in the sunlight. It momentarily picks daisies, accidentally

(oops) drowns an innocent girl, orders some random
smart-bombings for good measure, and then, in a vengeful
    rampage,
kidnaps the mad young doctor and carries him to the old mill.

Ah, the old mill, classic symbol of American industry.
The villagers find the girl's body floating in the river and
instinctively light torches, for suddenly it is night again, and
the villagers surround the mill, as villagers will.
The windmill spins and the waterwheel spins as the villagers,
thirsty for vengeance, amass, their torches raised. They set
the old mill ablaze as the now remorseful young doctor
awakens just in time to hear the monster say "I'm sorry,
I'm dreadfully sorry, I didn't mean it, ask not why the torch
has been passed, I will not accept my party's nomination,
I'm not a crook, I'm just a klutz, I lusted in my heart,
mistakes were made, read my lips no new taxes, I did not
have sex with that woman, Iraq did too have WMD's,
these banks are too big to fail, and all I want is for you
to love me, please love me, I wanna be loved by you, just you,
and nobody else but you," as the flames rise and the old mill
crumbles and the monster, "poo-poo-pee-doo," that glorious
executive beast disintegrates while the credits roll
to the tune of "Happy days are here again / The skies above
are clear again / So let's sing a song of cheer again /
Happy days . . . are . . . here . . . a . . . gain."

After a TCM War Movie Marathon

Now, this is what Memorial Day is about—
sitting on the sofa watching the daylight re-bombing
of Tokyo, the frightened but valorous Allied troops
re-landing at Omaha Beach on the foggy morning of
June 6, the lumbering Sherman tanks somehow
re-rolling towards Berlin in the Battle of the Bulge,
the wise-cracking POW's re-tunneling under
the clueless guard towers and barbed wire of the stalag,
smudged faces and Brooklyn dialects outsmarting
the Krauts once again—all the bravery and treachery,
wisdom and folly of a war well-fought, honorably won,
and cheered from the safe and sanctimonious perch
of historical distance. My personal favorites are
the submarine flicks. How many times have I watched
the grizzled, psychotic captain refuse the sensible advice
of his young first officer, or the scene where all
the enlisted men stacked like sardines in their bunks
read letters from girls back home, and the one short, smarmy
kid whose cousin was killed at Pearl and brother
you-better-believe he's gonna get him a piece of them
dirty Japs, or the against-all-odds, fire-all-torpedoes attack
in dangerous waters, the enemy depth charges
like huge garbage cans exploding close enough to rock
the sub, spitting rivets and opening torrents of icy water,
the crippled sub sinking to the rocky bottom,
the anxious faces of the crew as they listen
for the radar ping, and the much-despised college-boy ensign
who's crazy idea saves the whole crew from certain death?

Give me on Memorial Day the battle-weary voice
of Clark Gable, the rugged idealism of Burt Lancaster,
the crazy charm of Glenn Ford, the vulnerable heroism
of Van Johnson, the fierce loyalty of Ernest Borgnine,
even the loveable arrogance of Charlton Heston.

How thrilled I am to see once again the crafty,
crippled U-boat sneak through the gap in the anti-sub nets,
weaving its way miraculously between mines, thrilled
when the periscope pops up in the midst of Japanese
Destroyers, Aircraft Carriers, Troop Transports, and Battleships.
Something wonderful there is about ordinary men
in unbearably close quarters, under impossible circumstances,
facing the challenge of their lives, that brings to the surface
the worst and the best in humanity. How rare
and beautiful indeed when the wounded and
deranged captain sees the target he's chased halfway
across the Pacific appear suddenly within range.
It's a story he'll tell later only to those
able to appreciate it. He sends off the final torpedo,
mouthing a prayer as it shoots forth. Then the silent
satisfaction before the jubilation as through
the periscope he sees the ships begin to blow,
one by one, in chain reaction. "Scope down.
Right standard rudder. Steady as she goes." Then it's
back to Pearl, to medals and parades, to the women
waiting, to the whole incredible post-war boom,
to us, the babies who would grow up in their shadows,
celebrating and mourning the world gone by.

Transportation

Everybody agrees that cobblestones
are pretty but painful. Horses
also hate them. The lovely rattle
of hooves and carriage wheels
is merely ear candy for movies.
Only chiropractors secretly adore them.
A likely story, don't you think?
You may already know that
Ronald Colman believed with all
his celluloid heart that the story
revolved around him. Who could argue
with a voice like honeydew melon?
It's entirely possible that this life
is all about blade skill—foil, epee, sabre.
It's also possible that this life
is all about tongue skill—the passionate
whisper of vows in your lover's ear
on London Bridge under a gibbous moon.
Cut. Print. That's a wrap.
Kill the lights. Strike the set.
Wave once for me, my lovely,
to the guard at the gate. The exit
is so much quicker than the entrance.
Though painful, the yearning conveyed
by the old train's midnight whistle
is pretty indeed. Think of me,
won't you, when you hear it cry?

Graham Greene Fever Dream

For years he had kept a revolver
in the top drawer of his desk.
And now he sat in the dark, heavy
with guilt; cheap Scotch seeped
through his pores as he rolled
bullets through his fingers.
He was thinking of his wife
and his young mistress;
a small statue of the Virgin and Child
observed him from the desktop.

If only his wife had acted
upon her lust and left him
for his young assistant, he would
not feel so alone now. If only
his young mistress had not been
quite so fixated on his fatherly virtues
when she had sought him out
during the night of the blackout.
She was too young not to be impressed
by the menial job of a colonial policeman
in a small West African village.
Why had he praised her idiotic
stamp collection? Why hadn't his friend
the priest given harsher penance or,
better yet, sent him into holy exile?
"Each man must find his own way
through this purgatorio," he had said—
a watered-down substitute for consolation.

In the movie he'll be played
by Trevor Howard, whose melodious voice
will make it all sound so beautifully tragic.
Rita Hayworth will not dance the Hoochie-koo.
The only erotic relief in this picture
will be the awkward seduction scene
back in Act One when the girl—yes, she's
really too young to call a woman—innocently
compliments his looks, his intelligence,
and his bravery as the Freudian rain
pelts the tin roof. It's all one inevitable
elegiac fall from that dark and stormy night
until the trigger is pulled and the music rises.

For years he had kept a revolver
in the top drawer of his desk.
And now there he sat, finally feeling
himself at the heart of the matter,
alone in the dark pushing bullets
into chambers. In only a few moments
he would drain the Scotch, rise,
and go out to perform his evening rounds
in the grimy village that had never really
become home for him, the loaded revolver
heavy in his side pocket. He would
easily find a gang of rowdy youths
in a fistfight to make it all look
like something good he had attempted—
something purely in the line of duty.

Farewell, Richard Brautigan

In the big, drafty house in Bolinas
you set yourself down in a chair
in front of your favorite window as
the wild Pacific raged against the shore.

The ghost in the corner bedroom
shimmered but never spoke to you.
Trout in hand, she only waved goodbye.

Out one day to shoot birds, you and I.
Somehow you turned the gun on me.
You thought I followed you to San Francisco.
I never did any such thing, Richie.

Like ashes from a bonfire, I only floated up.
For tickling the trigger, I forgave you long ago.
I wave my trout now like a banner in the breeze.

In the big, drafty house in Bolinas
you set yourself down in your chair.
Finally you turned the gun on yourself.
(The critics can't reach you now.)

I stand at a distance on the dunes, looking in,
trout in hand, waving hail and farewell, while
the wild Pacific rages against the shore.

Note from Pharaoh's Mother

Please excuse my son from ruling the Empire today.
He's not feeling well. He was up all night again
arguing with that shameful Hebrew slave Moses,
who has brought my son such headaches, you can't believe.
The court magicians have gone on strike,
and the healing waters of the Nile still have traces
of blood in them. I've still got frogs and gnats and
locust falling out of the closet every time I open it.
Where is this man's mother, I'd like to know?
Who would let such a wisenheimer loose upon
the world with his pushy tone and his one true God?
I'd like to go upside his head with the scepter of Amun-Ra.
Enough already. I'm sending Junior back to Karnak
the minute that final obelisk goes up. If those lousy
midwives had done their jobs we wouldn't be in this position.
You just can't get good help anymore. Ask the Mycenaeans,
they'll tell you. I'll try to have him back on the throne by Monday.

Pig in a Dutch Oven

If you visit the Tower of London
you will see Henry VIII's suit of armor,
and perhaps you will be amazed,
as I was, that a man known for gluttony
in his later years could be stuffed
into that well-polished little suit.
The image of a bloated, late-career Elvis
springs to mind, holding his breath
while his handlers zip him
into the famous bejeweled jump suit.
And like Elvis being ushered to his stool
during the stage blackout, Henry
being lowered onto his horse from a crane
would be funny if it weren't so sad.
Sometimes even the animal best-suited
for survival is conquered by the very
appetite that drives him to success.
Think of Macbeth, Richard Nixon, or
(I'll just go ahead and say it) you and me.

Hamlet on the Ash Heap

How weary, stale, flat and unprofitable
Seem to me all the uses of this world!
   Act 1, scene 2

Claudius was right about one thing: the clouds
still hang on you, young prince. It's been more
than a while now since my own father died,
and the bright, colorful dream coat the world once
slung so cavalierly over its shoulder still lies
in the mud. What can you do? *Get over it*,
say mum and uncle Claude. *It's been a month,*
after all. We've moved on. Why can't you?
You with your dark moods remind them
in moments undulled by drink that they, too,
balance on the battlements, and at any time
they might fall—or be pushed—to their end
on the rocks below. This life is all about grief,
is it not? There's Job sitting on the ash heap
after losing everything, wishing he'd never
been born, the bitter voice of his wife pleading
for him to curse God and die. How long did he
sit there, after all, before his three useless friends
dragged him off to the land of existential debate?
If Beckett had written the story, he might've
shown a queue of similar losers next to
the ash heap, with clothespins on their noses
and numbers in their hands like at the deli counter.
And Job, as he finally rose, might've muttered,
Next. There is no voice in your whirlwind, Ham,
and it's annoying to have you moping around
the castle in your black leathers with your
Nietzsche tucked under one arm, mumbling
about slings and arrows, bare bodkins, and
unweeded gardens. You with your PBS

conscience. Hike up your tights and pay attention.
Your choice is ours: we must either act or die.
You may have heard this somewhere before
(maybe in a John Ford movie): dying is the easy part.

Totemic

She heard the rumble of distant thunder.
Clouds roiled overhead as the sky grew dark.
She lifted the big umbrella and it sprang open
just as the clouds broke. Blood rained

from the sky, pouring over the edges
of the umbrella like a waterfall. She walked
down the middle of the deserted street.
She walked past the bank and the coffee shop,

past the hardware store and the elementary school.
The street was filling up with blood;
her shoes were now stained. A large brown bear
ambled out of the drugstore. He turned and

said to her, *Your only hope is to keep walking.*
His thick coat was matted with clotted blood.
Soon the street was a shallow red river.
The sky crackled and sparked. She followed

the bloody current to a place that had been
an important intersection. A grocery store had stood
on one corner, a car wash on another,
the police station on another, medical and

dental offices on another. The river deepened here
and poured over the edge of the broken asphalt,
falling into a pool below. A pink mist rose up
around the base of the falls. White salmon breached,

straining to leap the falls, dropped back under.
The large brown bear sat on his haunches
in the pool, feasting upon the white salmon.
It could be worse, he said. *This could be you.*

He caught another salmon in his claws and devoured it.
The wind tugged at her. The rain turned to hail—
small red pellets pelted her umbrella. She began to
wonder just how long the umbrella would hold.

V. Thirst No More

In Monet's Garden

Strolling there at the time of the evening breeze,
you begin to comprehend the movement he
godfathered. It really is all about the light—
how it filters through the greenery, how it
shimmers on the lily pond, illuminating
the numerous flowers, how it softly bounces
off the walls of the famous yellow house.
Stand in that house, in practically any room—
the humid little kitchen, the spacious
sitting room smothered in Japanese art,
even the old man's upstairs bedroom—
and gaze upon the scene that inspired the life
that inspired the work—painting after painting
a new attempt to capture that light as it
awakened every living thing. Listen
to the birds, the cool buzz of the insects;
smell the bread baking in the oven.
It's not difficult to imagine Monet himself
at his window, a beneficent smile
obscured by the long, gray whiskers,
surveying his own private piece of paradise.
After so many centuries crouched in the shadows,
holding our fig leaves in place, it's difficult
but perhaps necessary to imagine ourselves
walking upright, naked, and unashamed
in that gracious light—no more birth pangs,
no more thorns and thistles—only the goodness
of the garden and the delight it brings
to the senses as they break open into full blossom,
in Monet's garden, where no serpent slithers
along the rim of the pond, and no angry cherubim
swings a flaming sword across the garden's gate.

To Vincent on His 158th Birthday

After a long, wet, dreary, dark, lonely,
sickly winter, spring has finally arrived.
I'm sitting at a café table with a boiled egg,
cheese, and fruit. For the first time in months
my head is clear and my heart is content.
I hiked up to Hunter's Point yesterday.
Remember the hawks we watched up there
last summer as they rode the wind currents
along the hillsides? One flew directly at me,
then glided over, close enough that I could
see the black and white pattern on his tail feathers
and the shock of red around his shoulders,
close enough to meet his eye before he soared
over into the ravine, where he circled awhile,
finally perching atop a tall pine. I didn't have to
wish you were there because you were, just as
I have stood beside you in certain wheat fields,
looked over your shoulder at bouquets of
sunflowers, sat on a straw-bottomed chair
in a bright, spare, crooked bedroom. These
moments draw most of the poison out of the wound.
In time, the wound heals over. A scar toughens
the flesh on the outside while, with luck and work,
the soul softens within. Some of the poison lingers
in the bloodstream; eventually it will hit
the heart like a clot. Until then, we have
the café table in the shade, the hawks
on their winding paths, the pictures that invoke
beatific light, even those lit only by
pale stars and a withered moon. Especially those.

Gymnopédies

I

Imagine Erik Satie playing the piano in a corner
of Le Chat Noir, Montmartre, Paris, circa 1888.
In another corner, Debussy nurses his cognac.
George Auriol doodles at the next table.
Parisians come and go in top hats and splendid
dresses, ever in a state of sophisticated languor.
Below, the Seine flows. Doves coo in the awning.
Ravel will wander in not long after midnight.
The garcon pours a row of glowing absinthe.

II

Satie leans on one elbow and begins to touch
the keys as if for the first time. Knowing that
it matters to no one, or practically no one,
he begins to orchestrate the falling of the leaves
as they swirl in the late afternoon breeze.
And why not? Knowing that his little game
matters not a whit, that in fact nothing, or
practically nothing, depends upon such things,
he is free to daydream this small disjointed melody.

III

Debussy leans his head back and closes his eyes.
Auriol lifts his pen and turns toward the music.
"Wagner can stew in his sauerkraut," Satie
once said to them. And in the dreamy half light
of Le Chat Noir, on an autumn afternoon,
Debussy is inclined to agree; he is, you might say,
lulled into a lavish and sublime melancholia
from which he may never recover. And you? Will
you not also give way to the falling of the leaves?

Cat's Cradle

On a serigraph by Ben Shahn

Wrapped loosely in delicate strings, the pudgy
fingers face one another like kidnap victims
who have just awakened from an ether
fogbank and found themselves bound together
on the dusty floor of an old saw mill.

Entranced, the fingers of the left hand
and the fingers of the right seem to stare
across the small space between them. Perhaps
they are thinking: What lazy spider
has looped us together like this?

What is very soon to happen will at first
appear as utter chaos: the rollicking
fingers jerking and bobbing, poking and
pulling, like some wild, swirling
Kung Fu street demonstration.

But in Shahn's drawing he captures the moment
just before the transformation begins:
the fingers suggest those of a violinist
poised above his instrument in the instant
before the conductor's baton begins its dance.

Begging Bowl

Seeing the poem printed below his name
in a prominent magazine, the poet somehow
convinces himself that the poem is in fact
his own creation. He believes that his hours
of hard work—the joyful labor of pushing words
around on the page, of pacing out the lines
and listening to alternate rhythms—
have earned him the right to call the poem his.
How soon he forgets the mid-winter morning
of the poem's birth, when he had lurched
out into the cold, splintered begging bowl
in hand, and stumbled into the marketplace,
his belly empty as an old wineskin. And
how quickly he replaces the face
of the old merchant who took pity on him,
the wrinkled and weathered face of the one
who lifted a paddle of steaming rice
into his meager bowl, with his own face.
Somehow between that gracious moment
and this, the poet devised the heretical fiction
of himself planting the rice kernels, cultivating
the paddy, harvesting the crop, then
cooking the rice over an open fire on the night
of a full moon. But you and I both know
that even as he reads the poem now printed
below his name in a prominent magazine,
the old emptiness in his belly returns, and
the poet, like a supplicant at some ancient altar,
silently holds forth his little wooden bowl.

Fool in the Attic

Go ahead, try to ignore him, that
gregarious wise guy in your head.
Try as you might to bring your body
under the discipline of the breath
and use it as a drill to dig a well
to the soul, again and again his
incessant chatter will haul the bucket
back to the surface. The Buddhists
call him Monkey Mind, recalling
the numbing scat of our hairy relatives
in the canopy as we walk through
the jungle of the post-modern world.

What he wants more than anything
is to see you climbing awkwardly
into the trees after him, narrowly
missing his tail as he leaps
from branch to wagging branch,
mocking you with his screeching
and wailing. Again and again
you must return your gaze back
to the path before you. Again and ever
again turning back, turning back,
imagining a Someday when the nerves
in your legs don't ache to follow him.

No Lights, No Siren

Billy Wilder knew what could happen
if the devil grabbed hold of your heel:
no matter how bright, how handsome,
you could end up floating face down
in some rich old broad's swimming pool
with the paparazzi snapping photos
as they drag you from the green water and
haul your soggy corpse away. Even if
you get to tell the juicy details of
how you got there in classic Hollywood
flashback form, you still, in the end, get there.
The heavy ambulance doors swing shut;
the tires roll down the crunchy gravel driveway.
Nobody even notices as you make
the final turn onto Sunset Boulevard.

News Item

Forty-two. That's the exact number
of two-inch metal sewing needles
that doctors found in the torso
of a two-year-old boy in Salvador, Brazil.
Today the doctors removed the four
most dangerously-placed needles,
leaving the rest for further operations.

In the x-ray the needles light up
like iridescent icicles in the dark.
The boy's stepfather inserted the needles
under the direction of his entranced
girlfriend as part of a month-long
Candomble ritual designed to hold
the stepfather and his girlfriend together.

And still there are those who insist
that humans are evolving into
more advanced creatures, leaving
further and further behind our old
predatory nature with each new generation.
Try explaining this to the boy's doctors
as they remove the other thirty-eight needles.

A Kind of Pilgrimage

Walking down a rocky path
I focused on a single smooth white stone
until I became that stone.

Feeling a snake coil around me
to take for himself my warmth
I became the snake.

When the circling hawk
grabbed me in his talons
I became the hawk.

Swooping over a field
I was struck by a hunter's bullet
and dropped from the sky.

I lay again on a rocky path
until I turned once again
into a single smooth white stone.

And there I stayed
gleaming in the midday sun
until you picked me up.

Credo at 37,000 Feet

Most of my friends are strident atheists
of the snide, neo-Dadaist tribe;
they find it difficult not to smirk and snort
at the mere intimation of immortality.

Some of my friends fall into the post-Marxist
camp of toothless Taoists with a twist of Zen;
to make them happy, sit them on a buckwheat
zafu and point them roughly eastward.

Gothic spires only fill them with dread.
My seat-mate on this flight has already
ordered two vials of vodka and poured them
into Diet Coke. She confesses her belief

that if she doesn't imbibe, the plane will fall
right out of the sky. Well, we all have our
different ways to cope. Me, I have these
prayer beads I roll across my knuckles.

These days I am straight-up blood of Christ.
Pipe organ me. Wafer me. Plop me down
before a crucifix and hymn me while
I murmur halos and color-stained light.

Swing the incense my way; splash me please
with holy water and speak to me of seeds
planted in good soil and vines that abide,
of water into wine and prodigal feasts

with golden rings and fatted calves.
We all admit that nowadays it is hard
to be certain of anything. Is the planet
suffering a menopausal hot flash

or just going through a second adolescence?
Is the famous saint another sinner in disguise?
Like smoke from a pile of smoldering leaves,
our souls meander through the autumn twilight.

My seat-mate and I toast a bon voyage.
Along with the beads and the vodka,
we hope our shy heavenward whisperings
weave a spell that keeps this jet aloft.

Ode to St. Anthony of Egypt

Of all the saints, my Anthony,
I love you best. For you did
what I long to do: you walked away
from a life of comfort and ease,
walked away from the green Nile valley
out across the sand and into the
desert of the human heart.
Alone, you dug out a cell,
blew a kiss to the mad world,
and tucked yourself in for the long soul's night.
And when the demons came,
as demons will, you fought them off
with the sign of the cross and the sweet
name of Our Lord—the name that
nourished you when there was no bread,
the name that moistened your lips
in a dry and barren land.
Anthony, I can count the ribs
just beneath your cracked skin,
the whiskers hang down like dried seaweed,
the dirt and dust cake your every wrinkle.
Come, let me guide you down to the river
where I may wash you, and oil your skin,
and trim your nails and tie back your hair.
Anthony, Anthony, sit on this rock with me
and tell me how it is to lose so much,
and then to give what's left away,
and then to forget what's been lost and given
in the good and strong arms of Our Lord.
Here, let me place some honey on your tongue.
Can you yet hear the water trickling
down the dim back wall of your cave?
This steady stream that kept you alive,

that overflowed your cupped hands,
the stream that ran beyond your humble cell,
filling first the desert within and then without,
the stream that still flows on and on,
my Anthony, even though you're gone.
This stream of living water from which
I now sip and thirst no more, I offer to you,
reader, in memory of this beloved saint.

About the Author

David Denny grew up in the suburban beach communities of southern California. He studied theatre and literature at Golden West College and California State University, Long Beach. He moved north for a short time, earning an MFA in creative writing at the University of Oregon. Later, he received an MAT degree from Fuller Theological Seminary. He currently resides in the San Francisco Bay Area with his wife, a prominent choral conductor and music teacher. They are the proud parents of two talented children and the guardians of a persnickety cat named Molly Bloom. Denny is Professor of English at De Anza College and former editor of *Bottomfish* magazine. He is the recipient of a 2013 Artist Laureate award by the Arts Council of Silicon Valley, and for two years he served as inaugural Poet Laureate of Cupertino. His poems and short stories have appeared in numerous literary magazines and journals, including *Atlanta Review*, *California Quarterly*, *Iodine Poetry Journal*, *Pearl*, and *The Sun*, among others. His chapbook, *Plebeian on the Front Porch*, was published by Finishing Line Press in 2012. When not writing or teaching, he can often be found watching classic movies from the balcony of the Stanford Theatre.

4221888R00067

Made in the USA
San Bernardino, CA
06 September 2013